THE COLOR OF COLOMBIA

THE COLOR OF

COLOMBIA

PUBLISHER
Santiago Montes Veira

LAYOUT AND DESIGN
Angélica Montes Arango
Pedro Nel Prieto Amaya
Santiago Montes Veira

PHOTOGRAPHY
Germán Montes
Stephan Riedel
Miguel Morales
Fredy Gómez
Hernán Díaz
Peter Goodhew
Héctor López
Angélica Montes
Andrés Hurtado
Luis Hernán Garcés
Natalia González
Francisco Forero
Archivo I/M Editores

TEXTS
Helena Iriarte Núñez

TRANSLATION
Peter Goodhew

PHOTOMECHANICS
Gabriel Daza L.

PRINTING
Editorial Nomos S. A.

© I/M Editores Ltda.
Apartado aéreo 89499, Bogotá, Colombia

ISBN 958-97339-2-1

CONTENTS

POLYCHROMATIC COLOMBIA

By Alfredo Iriarte

THE pages of this book are an impressive journey the length and breadth of a vast collection of works which, carved by the overpowering forces of nature and forged by the inspired and patient handiwork of men, make up this fascinating place called Colombia. From the beaches at sea level to the heights at which *frailejones* rear their crowned heads through the mist, one perceives the unmistakable magic that the tropics imbue in all that is born, grows and develops, which in short could be defined as a supreme and stunning empire of color, whose exuberant presence impacts us as much in the plumage of birds as in the majesty of the plant life.

In Colombia, on a par with the marvels of the flora and fauna, rivers, valleys and Andean massifs, are the miracles created by anonymous pre-Hispanic sculptors, goldsmiths and potters who corroborated Jorge Zalamea's memorable epithet that in the arts and literature underdeveloped peoples have never existed. Thus we see the perfect works of the goldsmiths of the Tayrona, Sinu, Quimbaya, Muisca, Calima, Tolima and other cultures, together with the no less admirable works of ceramists and potters of the same origin, and with inescapable amazement we return to the fascinating mystery of the Agustinian megaliths, whose twin-headed gods, fanged warriors and eagles grasping serpents still challenge, in their stony silence, the curiosity of the most experienced researchers behind an armor-plating of inscrutability, comparable only to that of the gigantic heads that stare at the infinite from the the island of Pascua.

Together with Mexico, Ecuador, Peru and Bolivia, Colombia has the privilege of possessing incomparable treasures that for three centuries, between the Discovery of America and Independence from Spain, were fashioned by both Spanish and native architects, sculptors, wood carvers and painters of religious art. These five nations, and Brazil in Portuguese America, are the fortunate and exclusive home to this fantastic American Baroque, notably enriched and revitalized in comparison to European Baroque, thanks to the multitudinous presence of Indian flora and fauna that adorn the golden universe of the reredos and the mural paintings that decorate the ceilings and walls, many of which have come back to life thanks to the surgical work of talented restorers.

These marvels of American Baroque, before which we can remain for hours and hours without tedium or fatigue, are a prodigious combination of three influences:

- The European, contributed by artists, mostly religious, who came to these kingdoms from Spain.

- The Mudejar, that arrived by the same means and is the result of a vigorous style that marked Arabian art in Spain. In our churches and monasteries, and in many civic buildings, this influence can be easily discerned, with a completely Mudejar example being represented by the church of San Francisco in the city of Cali.

- The indigenous, a specially clear and vigorous style that, as we mentioned earlier, is expressed by the tumultuous presence of flora and fauna, as well as by the sharp

Indian and *mestizo* features that are found in many of the carvings and paintings left by vicereine art, a superb example of which is the canephoros that initiates the stairs of the pulpit of San Francisco, in Popayán.

Great Spanish-American Baroque is essentially an art of catechism, conceived and executed to the supreme end of supporting missionaries in their arduous evangelizing work. In todays terms, it was what we would call an efficient visual aid, since in its reredos, paintings, wood carvings and frescos are all the principal characters and decisive chapters of the Old and New Testament. But this does not mean that our Baroque is a particularly solemn art, gloomy and severe. On the contrary, apart from inevitable exceptions, it is a joyous and playful art, perhaps because of the multicolored presence of opulent South American nature.

Cartagena de Indias deserves a special mention in this preface. It was the most important port of the Spanish Empire in South America, the "outer wall and key to the kingdom", whose impressive system of defence is preserved almost intact, much more complete that the rest of the Indian cities that Spain had to fortify in order to protect them from the boundless greed of buccaneers. Here we wish only to draw the reader's attention to a strange phenomenon that we might well call an unusual case of involuntary beauty. The designers and builders of these castles, bastions, revellines and ramparts were exclusively military engineers for whom aesthetic intentions or projects did not form part of their terms of reference. Their only objective, fully achieved in practice, was to attain an impeccable defensive efficacy to the point of achieving complete invincibility, as occurred in Cartagena. However the marvel was that, in addition to their military and strategic plans, these engineers unintentionally gave shape to monuments that today attract us with the magnetism of their sober, simple and imposing beauty. And this example, although outstanding, is not the only one. Almost a millennium ago, in the Middle Ages, when builders of the walls of Ávila erected enormous towers at equal intervals along that imposing stone canvas, they not only succeeded in making the city impenetrable from attack by catapults and *sambucas* but also left us a monument of overwhelming beauty.

Making no concession to patriotism, it can be asserted that Colombian painting and sculpture during the last eighty years are outstanding in this hemisphere, including North America. And the same may be said of modern Colombian architecture. In the pages of THE COLOR OF COLOMBIA, readers can admire some of the most praiseworthy and significant examples of these three branches of fine arts that the masters have left us, which have justifiably achieved an international reputation.

Nature, and the past and present of the arts, harmoniously come together in the pages of this book, which offers Colombians and visitors alike a superb chromatic and aesthetic panorama.

PRIVILE

GED NATURE

ARM seas and white sandy beaches, snow–capped mountain peaks and shimmering plains, immense savannas crisscrossed by rivers, springs nurtured by mountain *páramos* and dense jungle make up the landscape of Colombia, a country situated in the tropics at the meeting of two continents, making it a privileged natural region.

Its broad coastal regions have a variety of climates, vegetation and indigenous cultures, which have developed their own ways of life and cultural expression. On the Pacific Ocean, the constant humidity maintains the lushness of unspoiled nature, and in the Caribbean, warm waters bathe a variety of coastlines that range from the dense vegetation of mangrove swamps to the arid deserts of the peninsula of La Guajira. From its coasts, which were the first regions to be colonized, the Spanish Conquerors began to explore inland following the course of the Río Grande de la Magdalena. They were looking for the legend of El Dorado and eventually reached the fertile highland plain of the Muisca Indians, where an abundance of resources and a favorable climate encouraged them to found Santa Fe de Bogotá, which was quickly to become the heart of the *Nuevo Reino de Granada*.

The rugged landscape of its three majestic *cordillera* and the Sierra Nevada de Santa Marta produces innumerable niches full of life: fertile valleys crossed by broad rivers, narrow canyons and steep hillsides on which dense forests abound, which on reaching the high plateaux, give way to lands that produced the basic foodstuff for the Indian inhabitants before the Spanish Conquest: corn. Above the cloud forests, paramos and perpetual snows produce the water that flows down towards the lands below.

The virgin forests of the Pacific coast and the Amazon are a refuge for thousands of species of fauna and flora, many of them unknown. The Indian tribes that inhabit the region preserve the myths, ancestral beliefs and way of life that have enabled them to keep their culture on the margin of civilization.

Colombia's relief ranges from perpetual snow peaks to hot deserts and can be divided into five broad regions: the Caribbean, the Pacific Ocean, the Amazon, the region of Orinoquía and the Andes mountains. Each possesses particular characteristics which together make Colombia a nation with one of the greatest biodiversity on Earth.

In this territory of contrasts, cultures have developed whose different ways of dealing with life and interrelating make up a world full of magic that is manifest in the color of Colombia.

THE MOUNTAINS

T HE Andes, the longest mountain chain in the world, thrown up by the collision of tectonic plates, extends like a great fan across Colombian territory and produces one of the most rugged landscapes in South America. Of the three mountain ranges, the central *cordillera* is the oldest and highest, whose snow–covered volcanoes of Huila, Tolima, Santa Isabel, Ruiz and many other peaks tower more than 5.000 mts. above sea level. Their intense volcanic activity has produced fertile soil in the *páramos* and cloud forests, on the slopes and in the valleys that separate the different mountain ranges.

The eastern cordillera is the widest, in which the fertile highland plain of Cundinamarca and Boyacá and the majestic Sierra Nevada del Cocuy are impressive landmarks, while the wettest páramos in the world constitute the region's water reserves. The western cordillera is the lowest of the three mountain ranges. Its slopes face the Pacific Ocean, an inhospitable region of dense jungle crossed by large rivers and which has the world's highest rainfall.

Since Colombia's mountains are situated in the tropics, landscape changes with altitude. On descending the mountain slopes from the cold highlands, the crops, flowers and fruits change, together with their fragrance and colors. The climate and the light become warm and the vegetation becomes lush.

The Sierra Nevada de Santa Marta is an independent mountain massif that has the highest snow covered peaks in the country.

The frailejón is the most common plant found in the páramo.

During the dry season, the
atmosphere is clear and the water
crystalline among the peaks of the
Sierra Nevada del Cocuy. Here a
few species exist that have adapted
to the extreme temperatures.

Otún Lake, in Los Nevados National Park of the central cordillera, is one of the many lakes that abound in the high mountain areas of Colombia.

The vegetation of the mountain páramos of Colombia is quite diverse, ranging from minute red ferns to clusters of enormous frailejones.

Tota Lake, the largest in the country, is situated in the department of Boyacá on a highland plain, close to the town Aquitania. The ecosystems of the cordillera permit a variety of flora and fauna.

Fúquene Lake is one of the largest in the valley of Ubaté and Chiquinquirá.

Water descends from the peaks of the central cordillera down deep canyons. Salto de Bordones in the department of Huila.

Wax palms, in the department of Quindío, are a national symbol.

Small plots of land fill the landscape with color in the south of the department of Nariño.

A considerable part of Colombia is covered by chains of mountains that fold one behind another until they fade into the horizon.

The desert of Tatacoa, in the department of Huila, is a beautiful, semiarid formation that preserves the fossil remains of prehistoric fauna.

The country's different climates produce a considerable diversity of butterfly species, of surprising shapes, sizes and colors.

Water is everywhere in Colombia, one of its attractions being waterfalls that cascade over rock faces and keep the environment humid, while parasitic species such as the orchid add color to the landscape.

At every altitude of the Andean region, including the lowlands in the foothills of the Llanos Orientales, nature expresses itself in all its splendor with enchanting tropical sounds and colors.

THE SAVANNAS

T O the east of the Andes, immense savannas spread out, the sunrise and sunset transforming the sky in an explosion of colors that light up the plains. The Llanos Orientales, spotted with mirity palms and forests along river courses, share with Venezuela the region's physical and cultural characteristics. Their inhabitants are cowboys who drive their herds across the savannas but also grow crops, especially rice. Large rivers and streams flow across these immense lands, providing irrigation for the rice paddies and an important means of transport.

The rivers of the Llanos Orientales, such as the Cusiana and Meta, are an important means of communication and resources for the region.

In the north of the country, the broad plains of Bolívar, Magdalena, Sucre, Córdoba and Cesar are fertile lands where traditional agriculture alternates with cattle ranching and where broad rivers spread their waters across the land to form innumerable *ciénagas*.

The wide valley of the Cauca River is covered by sugar cane plantations that produce the nation's entire output of sugar. The land is bathed by the Magdalena, a broad river that crosses the country from south to north, and the towns on its banks preserve their history and ancestral traditions.

The highland plains have a pleasant climate and are characterized by a serene landscape of small farms whose crops form a patchwork quilt of greens and browns, and villages that from the towers of their churches bear silent witness to the course of history.

From the foothills of the eastern cordillera, immense grassland plains extend towards the Orinoco River on the frontier with Venezuela, spotted with palm groves and river courses lined with tropical vegetation, in which the region's flora and fauna are concentrated.

Water surges over rapids on rivers in Tuparro National Park in the department of Vichada.

The fertile plains of the department of Cesar, a valley situated between the majestic Sierra Nevada de Santa Marta and the Serranía de Los Motilones, where the eastern cordillera terminates, are ideal for plantation farming and cattle ranching.

The department of Valle del Cauca, land of sugar cane plantations, is one of the most fertile regions in Colombia.

Rural dwellings spot the landscape of the highland plains of the departments of Cundinamarca and Boyacá and the rolling hills of Antioquia.

THE COASTS

The Caribbean and the Pacific Ocean have been a source of income for their inhabitants and important poles of development for the nation.

THE northern coast of Colombia possesses a variety of natural regions, such as the desert of La Guajira and Tayrona National Park, where rivers of crystalline waters flow into the sea from the foothills of the Sierra Nevada de Santa Marta. Here the vegetation is lush and the forests reach reach down to the beaches. Following the coast towards the west, there are innumerable bays of calm waters and white sandy beaches in between fishing villages and the cities of Santa Marta, Barranquilla and Cartagena, whose bay is still protected by fortresses built by the Spanish. Towards the Gulf of Urabá beaches and fishing villages are interpersed with mangrove swamps, the habitat of marine life and other species that live in their branches.

On the Pacific coast, one of the wettest places on Earth, where the Cuna, Embera and Katíos tribes maintain their customs, myths and legends, nature is wild and inhospitable. From the frontier with Panamá to *Cabo Corrientes*, the coastline is rugged, with innumerable cliffs, and towards the south it is low and susceptible to flooding. Between July and October, humpbacked whales reach the warm waters of the Colombian Pacific Ocean during the mating season, when the males emit their song to encourage the females to choose a partner.

The magic of the Caribbean islands is evident in the multicolored sea of the archipelago of San Andrés and Providencia, the most distant of the Colombian islands.

On the desert peninsula of La Guajira, the golden sands, the cliffs and the Caribbean come together in one of Colombia's most spectacular landmarks in Colombia: Cabo de La Vela.

The foothills of the Sierra Nevada de Santa Marta, the world's highest coastal mountain, sink into the sea at Tayrona National Park, forming colorful bays.

Rocky shorelines lined by lush jungle or immense mangrove swamps, such as those of the Ciénaga Grande de Santa Marta, make up some of the richest habitats in tropical Colombia.

The archipelagos of Rosario and San Bernardo, designated as national parks, are true paradises surrounded by numerous coral reefs that shelter colorful marine life.

Every sunset over the sea is a marvel of shapes and colors that invites us to engage in contemplation.

The Colombian Pacific coast,

wild and mysterious, is a

still undiscovered biological

universe.

Dense jungle borders the northern coastline of the Pacific Ocean. The foothills of the Serranía del Baudó form impressive cliffs sculpted by the waves.

The Colombian Pacific region is one of the wettest places on Earth, due its position at the confluence of cold currents flowing up from the south and warm currents coming down from the north.

JUNGLES AND FORESTS

THE Colombian Amazon and the Pacific coast are jungle regions isolated from the rest of the country, but are, however, crossed by innumerable rivers and streams that form a natural means of communication used by the Indian inhabitants. In these regions the tree canopy prevents the sun rays from penetrating, huge flowers devour insects, and rivers are full of piranhas, silver-backed fish and pink dolphins playing in the water. Thousands of birds deafen with their chatter and all kinds of animals live in trees and in niches beneath the floor of the jungle .

The Amazon, the largest river in the world, extends like a sea during the rainy season, giving a sense of grandeur and mystery to the region.

The abundant waters of the San Juan, Atrato and Patía rivers on the coastal hinterland of the Pacific flow through the wettest jungle on Earth.

Dense forests on the slopes of the Andes, the Sierra Nevada de Santa Marta and the Serranía de la Macarena shelter an abundance of endemic flora and fauna that occasionally includes an unknown species.

An impenetrable jungle covers much of Colombia, where perhaps like no other place on Earth, nature remains almost completely intact.

The Amazon River, which traverses the jungle, is the largest river in the world. Near Leticia, in the Colombian Amazon, it is two kilometers wide and as it approaches its mouth it becomes as broad as a sea.

In the Amazon jungle, trees tower fifty meters overhead, giant lotus leaves can support a person's weight, and rivers are populated by enormous snakes such as the anaconda and carnivorous fish such as the piranha.

Innumerable rivers and lakes make up the Amazonian basin and are the only means of communication for the Indian population and settlers who inhabit this region.

In the Serranía de la Macarena, the multicolored algae of Caño Cristales form one of the most beautiful natural phenomena in the world.

Colombia preserves much of its Andean forests, where the heat and humidity have produced a lush undergrowth in which a multitude of flora and fauna proliferate and interrelate.

Colombia is one of the world's richest countries in water resources, thanks to the considerable number of páramos found in its three cordilleras.

THE PEOPLE

LTHOUGH there is still a significant Indian population in the country, the majority of Colombians are *mestizos,* a mixing of Indian blood with that of other races and cultures, the descendants of the Spanish and slaves brought from Africa during the Spanish occupation. The characteristic that identifies them as a community is the fusion that occurred between these three worlds, creating a diversity that is evidenced in the particular forms of expression of the different regions of the country.

Each province possesses its own characteristics that range from the local accent, use of particular expressions and unique folklore, to its musical, literary and artistic production.

The inhabitants of the Caribbean, extrovert and cheerful, transformed the European accordion until it became characteristic instrument of the region that has given Colombia its most authentic music. The rhythms of the rest of the country have a marked Spanish influence, of which the *coplas* sung in the Llanos Orientales are among its richest expressions. There, the *joropo* sings about the land, work, animals and living freely.

Towards the east, in the Sierra Nevada de Santa Marta, two Indian groups, the Koguis and Arhuacos, descendants of the Tayrona civilization, fiercely preserve their culture, their customs, their ceremonial centers and their conception of the world. On the peninsula of La Guajira, with its hot desert and shimmering salt deposits, another Indian community, the Wayuu, proudly defends its ancestral traditions.

The inhabitants of the Colombian islands of San Andrés, Providencia and Santa Catalina in the Caribbean are populated by descendants of the English, African and Spanish. The

local architecture, diverse religious sects and a multilingual community are some of the characteristics of a culture that is different in every way from that of continental Colombia.

Several Indian groups live in the Pacific region of Chocó, together with others of African origin that were brought there to exploit the gold mines. The inhabitants of Popayán, capital of the department of Cauca, are proud to preserve their Spanish heritage. The inhabitants of the department of Nariño are predominately Indian, descendants of the Pasto and Quillacinga tribes. The majority of the country's cities are concentrated in the Andean region, while to the east lie the grassland plains of the Llanos Orientales, whose inhabitants played a decisive role in Colombia and Venezuela's struggle for independence from Spain. They are a free and enterprising people, closely attached to the land. The scarcely populated jungle of the Colombian Amazon is inhabited by Indian tribes, the majority of which have maintained their primitive way of life based on hunting, fishing and a growing a few crops, and are completely cut off from the rest of the country.

This is the mosaic of races and cultures of a nation that works hard to make a better life for its citizens.

A CHEERFUL AND LABORIOUS PEOPLE

By the sea-shore, under the clear sky and tropical breeze, the life of the coastal inhabitants is cheerful and peaceful.

THE rural inhabitant derives his living from fishing or farming, an activity that involves caring for a small plot of land together with his wife and children and also laboring on one of the nearby haciendas. In the many parts of Colombia, members of the family group devote themselves to craft-making that makes use of local resources: wool that they spin to make ponchos and blankets, which they sell at local markets or at craft centers in the city; clay with which they fashion beautiful objects, wood that they painstakingly carve or use to make musical instruments, and a variety of natural fibers that they have used since time immemorial. So between working the sea and the land, together with animal husbandry and crafts, the rural family makes enough to live on and produces a surplus to sell at the local village market. With the proceeds, its members buy the things they need at the village store, take a rest and talk about their misfortunes and joys, attend church and participate in local fiestas, and at sunset return to their land to prepare for another week of work.

The black communities that inhabit the Pacific coast have adapted to a natural environment that supplies them the resources for a full life.

For the Kogui Indians of the Sierra Nevada de Santa Marta, as for the inhabitants of other regions of the country, daily life is simple and in harmony with nature.

The river is an important means of communication, and in some remote areas is the only way for its inhabitants to travel and transport their products.

The Wayuu Indians that inhabit the peninsula of La Guajira are fishermen, shepherds or farmers who preserve their traditions, language and ancestral rhythms.

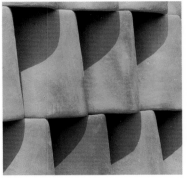

Most villages in Colombia produce a variety of crafts that incorporate locally available materials.

Since Spanish colonial times, Colombians have been deeply religious and worship is a basic part of life.

Thanks to a varied climate, the Colombian farmer reaps a broad variety of products for his subsistence and to supply the market.

On market day farmers take their products to town, and it is the occasion for get together and discuss their affairs over a cold beer.

The hearth continues to be the center of family life in both Indian and mestizo households.

ARTISTIC EXPRESSIONS

ARTISTIC expressions in Colombia go back several centuries before the arrival of the Spanish. The statues of San Agustín, the subterranean burial chambers of Tierradentro, and an immense legacy of pottery, gold and silver objects from the Indian cultures of Quimbaya, Sinú, Calima, Muisca and Tayrona, among others, constitute an invaluable part of the nation's heritage.

During the Spanish colonial period, goldsmiths and wood-carvers decorated churches with wonderful reredos, and artists painted images of saints and personalities of the times. The illustrations of the *Misión Corográfica* are remarkable, but the outstanding work are the meticulous drawings of the *Expedición Botánica*. During the XIX and XX centuries, many Colombian artists attained a notable place in the world of art.

As well as great art there is a rich tradition of craft-making, in which Indian and rural artisans apply techniques inherited from their forebears. The color, variety of materials employed, their shapes and usage, reflect the imagination of Colombians and the folklore of the tropics.

The Indians who inhabited the region of San Agustín, in the south of the country, populated a broad area with stone idols.

The development of pre-Hispanic gold working reached levels of considerable refinement.

The Indians of the Amazon create wonderful adornments that, apart from their decorative use, protect them from the evil spirits of the jungle.

The hands of the potter transform clay into pots that enshrine the earth spirit.

From La Guajira to the Amazon jungle and the southern Andean region, people weave with natural fibers dyed in bright colors: hammocks, hats, mochilas, ponchos, espadrilles and fabrics for making clothes.

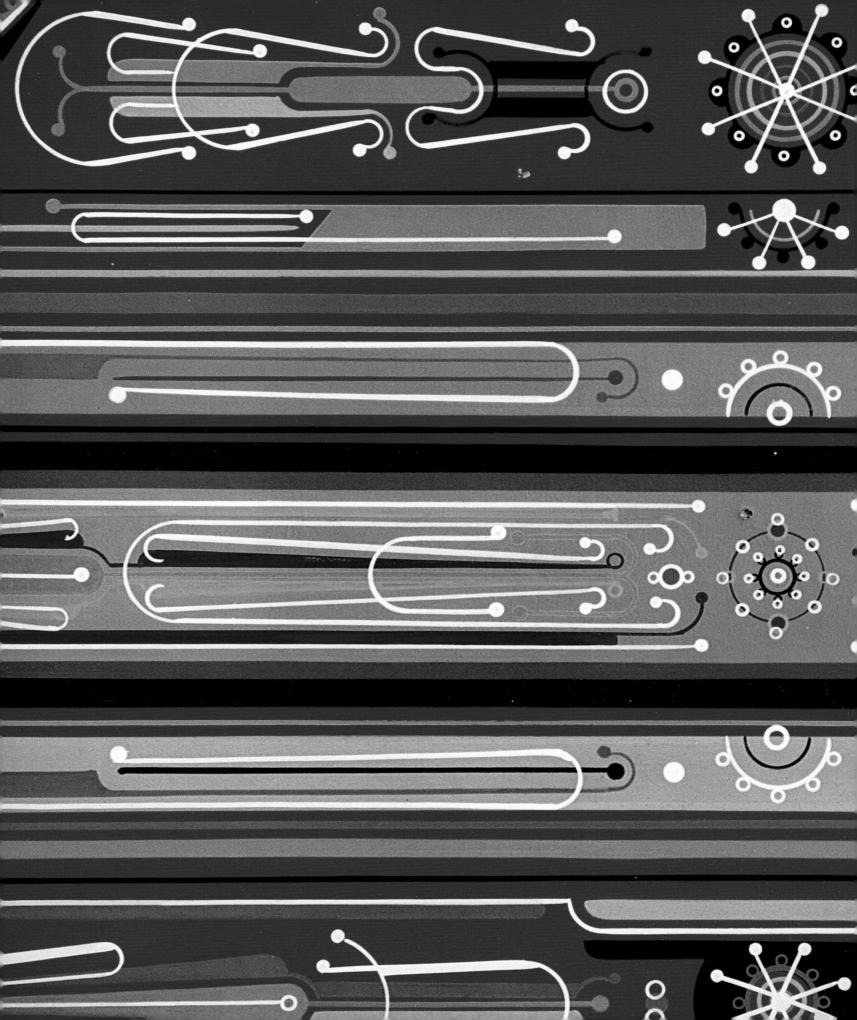

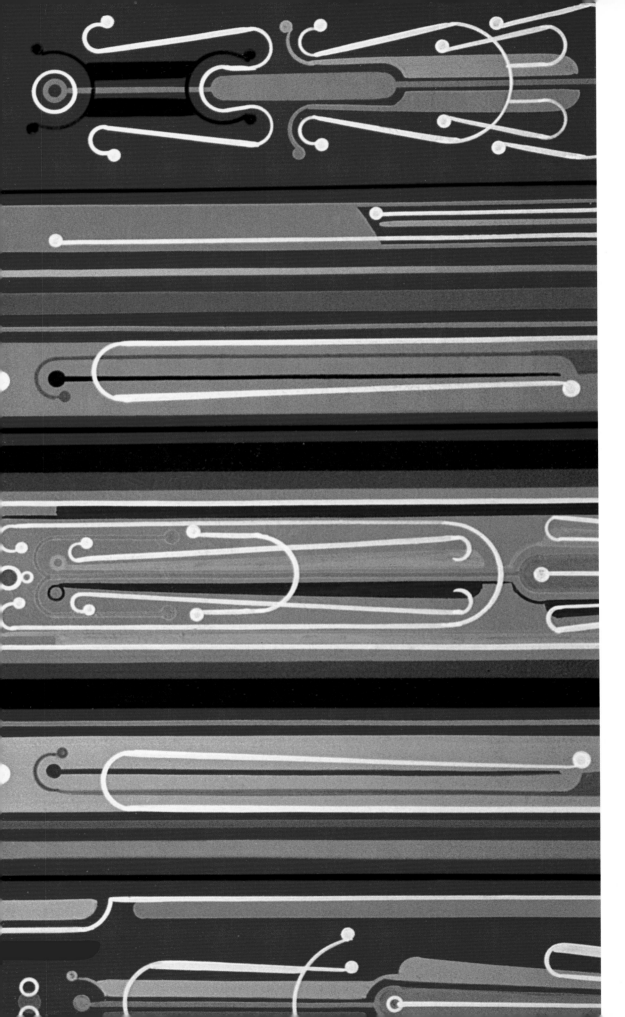

The fantasy with which the local buses are decorated fill the roads with color in the department of Antioquia.

After independence from Spain, architects of Spanish descent adorned the churches with techniques brought from the mother country, combined with the natural inspiration of Indian craftsmen.

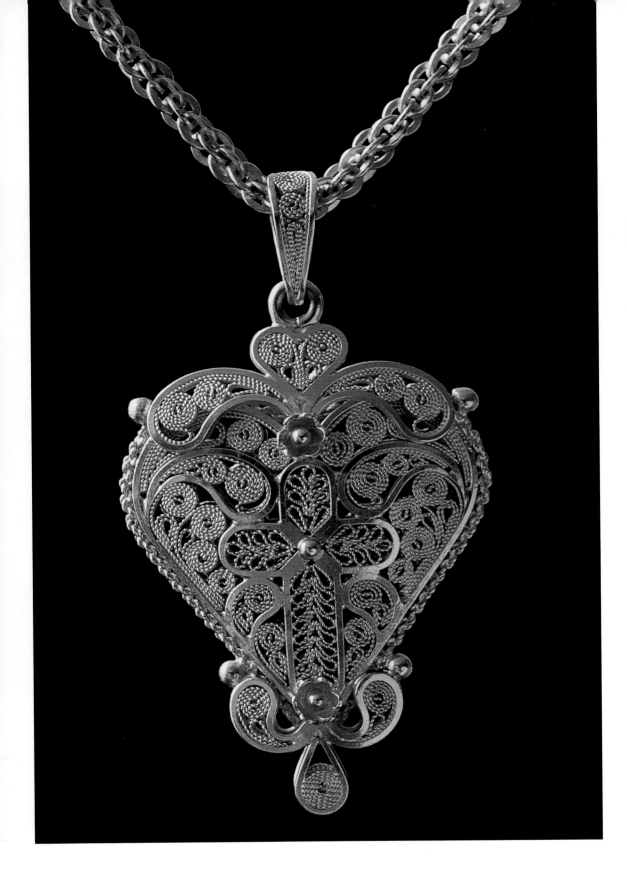

The Spanish colonial period left a legacy of valuable ornaments in gold, wood and stone that employed refined techniques still used in many parts of the country.

The public spaces of Colombian cities and the interiors of some of the buildings are decorated with art works from different epoques.

Fernando Botero, Rodrigo Arenas
Betancourt and many other artists
have contributed their works to
turn public spaces into museums.

FESTIVITIES AND CELEBRATIONS

The cheerful character of Colombians is reflected in their fairs and festivities full of music, noise and color.

COLOMBIAN people love celebrating. Religious and secular festivals take place throughout the country, although each region expresses its particular character.

The most important religious festival is Holy Week, the solemnity of which reaches its maximum expression in the towns of Popayán and Mompox. In addition to liturgical processions, some villages put on a dramatic representation of the Passion of Christ. Christmas maintains its traditional character, with carols being sung at home gathered around a nativity scene, seasonal dishes prepared and gifts placed beneath the Christmas tree. There are other festivals such as that of *San Juan y San Pedro* in the departments of Tolima and Huila, and those of the Magi and the Immaculate Conception, and every village celebrates its patron saint days and those in honor of the Virgin Mary.

Some of the popular festivities that take place include the carnivals of Barranquilla, *El Diablo* in Riosucio and the Blacks and Whites in Pasto; the *Correlejas* in the villages of the hinterland of the Caribbean coast, the *Cuadrillas de San Martín* in the Llanos Orientales, the fairs of *La Virgen del Rocío* in Manizales and the Sugar Cane Fair in Cali.

There are also cultural events such as the theater festivals of Manizales and Bogotá and the Poetry Festival of Medellín. In Colombia there is always a excuse to celebrate.

The joyfulness of the New Year

explodes in myriads of lights that

augur better days to come.

The Carnival of Barranquilla is the most traditional festival in the country that fills the city with music and color, and ends with the symbolic death of Joselito Carnaval just as Lent begins.

The cheerfulness of the inhabitants of San Juan de Pasto is expressed during the initial days of the New Year, when people paint themselves black and white and party on the streets.

There is always a reason to celebrate, whether it be a parade of Silleteros on the streets of Medellín or a patriotic festival. The important thing is for everyone to enjoy themselves.

In an explosion of music, cheerfulness and color, the Cuadrillas de San Martín incorporate diverse groups that represent Spaniards, Arabs, Indians and Blacks.

The religious fervor of Colombians is expressed in liturgical processions and celebrations during Holy Week.

Colombia's different ethnic groups preserve their particular cultural identity, as evidenced in their beliefs, traditions and dress.

TOWNS AND VILLAGES

The Tayrona culture built over 200 settlements in the Sierra Nevada de Santa Marta, some of which were veritable urban centers, such as the Lost City.

COLOMBIA is a nation of towns. Since the middle of the XVI century, with the founding of the first settlements, and up until the XIX century, with the colonization of the department of Antioquia, the creation of urban settlements did not cease and the majority became prosperous cities that today play an important role in the different sectors of the economy: industry, trade, agriculture, exports, goods and services, and in the different aspects of culture. The character of the towns is as different as that of their inhabitants. Some are proud of preserving their past, the traditions, customs and values that they inherited and which they are not prepared to change. Others were founded precisely from the need to open up new paths and possibilities that have characterized their constant transformation. Immigrants who settled in some regions of the country bringing their own culture with them have influenced the social composition of some regions.

Small villages have continued to be somewhat isolated and unaffected by transformations that have permitted economic and cultural progress in the rest of the country. On the other hand, they preserve the nation's ancestral memory and defend the past in the face of a supposed modernity that is eradicating the most valuable aspects of the national culture.

With the arrival of the Spanish
Conquerors, new building
techniques were imposed, such as
the use of clay tiles and mud walls.

Many villages in the department of Boyacá, such as Villa de Leiva and Ráquira, preserve their traditional structure, and the inhabitants paint the walls and columns with their notion of colorful harmony.

The Spanish colonial period left a legacy of innumerable villages throughout Colombia. Some of them attained importance at the time, such as Barichara in the department of Santander and Honda in the department of Tolima, whose historical sectors are kept in good repair.

As with all Spanish settlements, the churches and the civic buildings around the square played a fundamental role in the process of colonizing the new provinces. Santa Fe de Antioquia and Popayán are clear examples of the colonial architecture.

The town of Santa Cruz de Mompox, recently declared a World Heritage site, was one of the most important ports on the Río Grande de la Magdalena, the only route to the interior of the Viceroyship of Nueva Granada.

The class of city that the Spanish Crown wished to confer on Cartagena de Indias is noticeable in every detail of the most protected city in the New World.

The houses, balconies and fortresses of Cartagena, the walled city, constitute one of the most beautiful and best-preserved examples of colonial architecture in South America.

Villages founded during the colonization of Antioquia, such as Aguadas, preserve much of the urban layout inherited from the Spanish colonial period, but have adapted it to the rugged relief of the central cordillera.

Spanish and Republican elements are incorporated in the architecture of coffee farms, the houses being characterized by brightly painted corridors, balconies, windows and doors.

In cities such as Manizales,
Barranquilla and Medellín, elegant
buildings of the Republican period
are preserved, which in Colombia
developed at the beginning of the
twentieth century.

Bogotá, the capital of the Republic, has been the main urban center of the country since its foundation, and many of its buildings reflect the centralist nature of the governmental institutions.

Bogotá, like most Colombian cities, has entered the modern age and its buildings reflect the new life styles of its inhabitants.

The Fallen Christ of Monserrate, a carving of Christ that reposes in a church on the hill that dominates the nation's capital, bears loyal witness to the events that have taken place throughout Colombia's history and represents a symbol of hope for a better future.

PHOTOGRAPHERS

Germán Montes
Cover: A, B, F. Back cover: D. 30-31, 40, 43a, 48, 49a, 49b, 50, 62, 67a, 70, 71a, 73, 75b, 80-81, 83a, 91, 95a, 95b, 108, 111b, 114, 118, 120, 121b, 122, 123b, 124, 125a, 125b, 127a, 127b, 129a, 130, 131, 132, 133b, 135a, 135b, 136, 137a, 137b, 139b, 143b, 145b, 151a, 153a, 154, 155a, 155b, 156, 157a, 157b, 163b, 164, 166, 167b, 169a, 169b, 170, 171b, 173b.

Stephan Riedel
25a, 29b, 64, 92, 104, 105a, 105b, 106, 107b, 109b, 110, 116, 140, 141a, 143a, 151b, 159b, 161b, 171a.

Miguel Morales
25b, 31b, 34, 35b, 36, 37b, 39b, 43b, 45b, 47b, 77b, 79b, 81b, 83b, 129b, 150.

Fredy Gómez
Cover: C. Back cover: A, B. 18, 27a, 27b, 29a, 35a, 37a, 72, 74-75, 76, 85b, 97a, 97b, 112, 123a.

Hernán Díaz
78, 79a, 87, 89, 90, 126, 134, 139a, 141b, 142, 168, 172-173.

Peter Goodhew
28, 51a, 103, 113, 117a.

Héctor López
77a, 99b, 119b, 138.

Angélica Montes
14, 33b, 148.

Andrés Hurtado
44-45.

Luis Hernán Garcés
103b, 144.

Natalia González
Cover: E.

Francisco Forero
Cover: D. Back cover: F. 96, 100, 101a, 132, 145a.

I/M Editores
Back cover: C, E. 15, 16, 17, 19a, 19b, 20-21, 22, 23a, 23b, 24, 26, 32-33, 38, 39a, 41, 42, 46-47, 51b, 52, 54-55, 56-57, 58, 59a, 60, 61a, 63a, 65a, 66, 68, 69a, 82, 84, 85a, 93, 94, 98, 101b, 104, 107a, 109a, 115b, 117b, 119a, 128, 146, 147, 149b, 152, 153b, 158, 160, 161a, 162, 165a, 165b, 167a.